with strings

CHARLES BERNSTEIN

THE UNIVERSITY OF CHICAGO PRESS

CHICAGO AND LONDON

CHARLES BERNSTEIN is the David Gray Professor of Poetry an Letters at the
State University of New York at Buffalo. In addition to My Way, he is the author of
two collections of essays, A Poetics and Content's Dream, and more than twenty
books of poems, including Islets/Irritations and Rough Trades.

The University of Chicago Press, Chicago 60637
The University of Chicago Press, Ltd., London
© 2001 by Charles Bernstein
All rights reserved. Published 2001
Printed in the United States of America

10 09 08 07 06 05 04 03 02 01   1 2 3 4 5

ISBN: 0-226-04459-9 (cloth)
ISBN: 0-226-04460-2 (paper)

Library of Congress Cataloging-in-Publication Data
Bernstein, Charles, 1950–
With strings / Charles Bernstein
p. cm.
ISBN 0-226-04459-9 (cloth:alk. paper)—ISBN 0-226-04460-2 (pbk.:alk. paper)
I. Title
PS3552.E7327 W58 2001
811'.54—dc21   2001023362

♾ The paper used in this publication meets the minimum requirements of the American
National Standard for Information Sciences—Permanence of Paper for
Printed Library Materials, ANSI Z39.48-1992.

And they say
If I would just sing lighter songs
Better for me would it be,
But not is this truthful;
For sense remote
Adduces worth and gives it
Even if ignorant reading impairs it;
But it's my creed
That these songs yield
No value at the commencing
Only later, when one earns it.

– Giraut de Bornelh (tr. from French, 12th century)

contents

in place of a preface a preface

We used to say the artist would drop away and there would just be the work. Can we go further and say the work drops away and in its place there are stations, staging sites, or blank points of radical metamorphosis? Only when we experience this as an emplacement of textuality into material sensory-perceptual fields – turning ever further away from ideality in the pursuit of an ultimate concretion.

Art is made not of essences but of husks. Hazard will never be abolished by a declaration of independence from causality. But such a declaration may change how hazard is inscribed in our everyday lives.

As if to create not scales but conditions, not conditions but textures, not textures but projects, not projects but brackets, not brackets but bracelets, not bracelets but branches, not branches but hoops, not hoops but springs, not springs but models, not models but possibilities, not possibilities but plights, not plights but perceptual encounters, not perceptual encounters but live experience, not live experience but three-dimensional conundrums, not three-dimensional conundrums but philosophical buildings, not philosophical buildings but blind spots, not blind spots but virtual structures, not virtual structures but impossible necessities, not impossible necessities but pitchers, not pitchers but moldings, not moldings but pageants, not pageants but straddling heights, not straddling heights but conceptual rejoinders, not conceptual rejoinders but livid exponents, not livid exponents but cross-interventional convocations, not cross-interventional convocations but philosomatic trillings, not philosomatic trillings but blinking sensors, not blinking sensors but curtained encapsulations, not curtained encapsulations but plausibly deniable links, not plausibly deniable links but blinkered alarm, not blinkered alarm but ravishing dissuasion, not ravishing dissuasion but tripping tropes, not tripping tropes but embroidered fans, not embroidered fans but pillars, not pillars but mouthings, not mouthings but plasma, not plasma but branding lights, not branding lights but invented enclosures, not invented enclosures but sifting exposés, not sifting exposés but torque-topped initiations, not torque-topped initiations but philanderous moorings, not philanderous moorings but blurted secrets, not blurted secrets but curling capacities, not curling capacities but prismatic illocutions, not prismatic illocutions but pantomime, not pantomime but mourning, not mourning but placebos, not placebos but blistered ratiocination, not blistered ratiocination but inverting domination, not inverting domination but shifting fabrications, not shifting fabrications but tongue-tooled emanations, not tongue-tooled emanations but philogenerative groundings, not philogenerative groundings but blanket riveting, not blanket riveting but invested *détournement*, not invested *détournement* but . . .

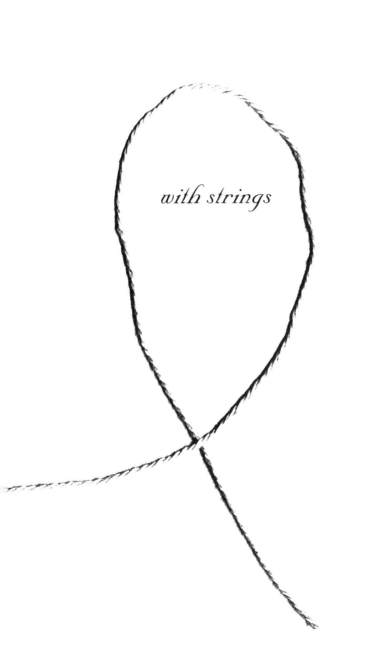

with strings

thinking i think i think

What are aesthetic values and why do
there appear to be lesser & fewer of
them? Quick: define the difference
between arpeggio & Armani. The baby
cries because the baby likes crying.
The baby cries because a pin is
sticking into the baby. The baby
is not crying but it is called
crying. Who's on first, what's
shortstop. The man the man declined
to be, appraised at auction at
eighty percent of surface volume.
Cube steak on rye amusing twist
on lay demo cells, absolutely no
returns. *Damaged goods are the only
kind of goods I ever cared about.*
The lacuna misplaced the ladle,
the actor aborted the fable. Fold
your caps into Indians &
flaps. Dusting the rigor mortis
for compos mentis. Rune is busting
out all over – perfidious quarrel
sublates even the heckling at
the Ponderosa. A bevy of belts.
Burl Ives turned to burlap. Who
yelled that? Lily by the lacquer
(laparotomy). *I'm here strictly on
business, literary business.* May
I propose the codicil-ready cables?
Like slips gassing in the night.
Chorus of automatic exclusions.
Don't give me no label as long as I
am able. Search & displace, curse
& disgrace. Suppose you suppose,
circumstances remonstrating. Crest

envy. Don't give me the Bronx
when you mean the Bronx. *This
one thing I know for she loathes
me so*: Ketchup will pass for blood
only under highly limited conditions.
I had a red ball / I watched it
fall. *Help me so that I may exist
again*. It's the billyclub not the
Billy that needs watching. Keep
your eye on the balloon (cartoon)!
Budge, but then move back into
position. In other words, steal
my car but don't steal my sister's
hood. Ironclad comeuppance. Breakfast
at the Eiffel tower, lunch at the
Kremlin, dinner at the Taj Mahal.
In other words, *hurt me
but don't hurt me so bad.*
May flies / So June can hold
July. That's no arrow that's a
diversionary tactic. That's no
spastic that's my elocutionary
lodge. When all the cares
have become little tiny porous
creatures, buckling under the weight
of the remorse. The barfly butters
his bread on all sides of the
collective agency, while even at home
the Colonel takes out the garbage.
*You will find a moist towelette
with your porridge.* Then just say so.
Cratylus, Cratylus, wilt thou be
mine? As I is the starch from
yesterday's yawning. *Cure me
so that I will smoke yet not be
consumed* (at least not at a
discount). *Pools rush in
where barriers have not been
fortified.* Rule rules
where furriers redesign. "Amish

modern." French poetry is looking
for a way out of "French poetry."
Ne touchez pas cette button. The
color of baloney. WWW.TheSirens.Org.
Ne touchez pas ma bologna. Her
hair was auburn her eyes like amber.
Honest to gosh gullies: arraignment
of a power untapped & untappable.
Quittez votre place (Kitaj dislikes
his place). Emboss my fiduciary
capitulations! The bellicose churning
of the unsettled stomach. *National
Geographic*'s "Robot" issue:
The Wilderness of the Future, e.g.,
the Gates Robot Preserve, the
American Robotic Conservancy,
the Fund for Robotic Culture,
the National Endowment for Robots
(a.k.a. U.S. Congress). Millions
for automation but not one cent
for elegy. Eight elephants dancing
deliriously to the wail of the
bumble bees. *So long, sailor /
goodbye failure.* Or let the pail
wear the head of the lotion. Here
is smoldering continuation. The
smell of green tea on Greene Street.
Bottled reticence. *Gimme gimme
gone.* Guilt in the form of guilt.

      "& even then my heart was aching
        For I am yours, just for the taking . . ."

ballad of blue green plate

This is an echoed house – speak loud &
your voice comes back to taunt. Evacuating
lesser known metonymics, cork-crusted
yet pining – full-throttled aviary
premonitions slashed to earth's moldering
omniscience – hurl of twice unfolded
manner – marbleized mannequins of ply-point
flush. Back off, re-spire, unswear

the latch, who purr unannounced like
lemons in a phase. The way to Unbetokened Bay
holds too many pores & hand executes
its own inhibition: wind for holes
to warp through, tunnels mixed with
rain, soaked by dawn's provisional spite.
Time to gather bows before the match
abandons plight. That undulates wacked-out

card players, figurines really, in tempo to –
sunken assurance & dug past, in which
acceleration ponders maze. Histrionics
suffuse the drunken hurricane. Preposterous
obligation, tuberous conundrums. Tones
in the basket of the baby's basket. *Because you
stole it but you're my friend & thank you.* Such
as the fire that. Long at loss unavailable to transparent

emulation. Pummeling as indecorously
as log floating mid-horizon. The soup
hot, syrup stickly, way unfoundering. Klieg
lights of the imaginary approximate the curtain
suffused with the unsaid, where telling tolls. Tattered
in astral fashion, such rips as become
the tears of what is unnamed because everywhere
pronounced. *That which* among whom between is sewn

aside the amidst, in of.

fiddle of the rat faced men

None goads the lure where spans
Receipt of song, floating on soldered
Trill as tools impose repair, slump
Old padre to your bloated core
Mine the tucks but not the pall
Autarkic buds have bid us gnaw

total valor

FOR & AFTER RÉGIS BONVINCINO

The spring came suddenly
Azaleas
But azaleas are a flower of the winter
We are not located in the space
São Paolo, New York, Santiago, San Francisco, Los Angeles
The wind is singing but it is not saying anything
Clouds seem to be sand there
Destiny of the navigators
"How provincial is São Paolo"
It's okay but in the evening it begins to ache
We were talking yesterday
      about how the fog
      sticks to the mountain
The best part is to depart

but pharaoh did not listen to moses

I place my arm on the armoire.
The minister frowns. The miser
recollects his days in Nice, mak-
ing creases. Slowly the gas leaks
from the plane. From the plane the gas
leaks slowly. The gas from the plane
slowly leaks. Polly puts the kettle on
what? But Pharaoh did not lis-
ten to Moses.

two places at once

Beyond the banal is the becalmed
Buffaloed majesty requiring a
Lighter for a filter, paradox
For 2-cents plain. Or landlubber become
Land grabber and the flab is all bucket
Of plenty in gabardine payback.
Baby make lots moolah, moxie
Irrefrangible overbite as County
Dare translates into biding time by the
Bric-a-brac. Boyish giggles toxify
Toy machines – burst umber bumbling
Even the sacrosanct tonnage
Loaded on the leveled playing field
Just above the rug pulled out from under.

captain cappuccino and his merry con leches

*I'm not telling you what you can't
do but what you can do.* The
station moves rapidly on the tracks
looking for the frame. Amid clangs
of threaded openings, barrage of having
known flickers acidly in the tell-tale
mirage of another way in. Ripple
of same that is always swapping
for marbleized fairy dust. But
let's not get sentimental. Go
blow, go below and examine the hypothesis
as it burns its way into the deep
structurelessness that buoys the
girls and makes men sweep. EXPECTORATE
IDEOLOGY: write piteously and deliver
yourself to sullen beauty, elliptical
judgments. Zeroing in for the spill.
Verb forms in the mouth, scum of sequence,
sentence, skirmish. Borders on asphalt,
your fault, my fault. Darting
in a delicious divertimento to
absent tablature, turbidity, luster.
Hearken to the choir of broken
wings – not the ones who
sing but the drawer on the other
side, open to the blank page
smudged with tacit misconstruals.
For if I delay it is not to
betray the secret writ in mars & furls
on the floor of the roiling
machine, funneled in flax.
Never (next to) coniferous
cohabitation, the principled pealing
that traps the aquatic ambiance
of the parasitic constabularies,

mystic launch of listening's
particle imagination. Blip
blip blip. Huddled against
percolation, futurity on the
bend, irritating (irrigating)
pitched surrender.

from talk alone you don't get a poem

It's your turn, Roger. The whole world's not nuts!
You earn your eye and the vastness vanishes
under the brick of an oily blanket,
only the doodles don't dare crack the count-
ing houses. Setting in motion something like
actuarial imbrication (hor-
tatory lamentation), as if bal-
looning bulbs. Say slither in the case of
presumptive hitherance – you know, the
tuck around the tootle, mickey mousing
with the last brass lunge. There are barbells in
the pantry, second shelf above the sag,
then a pound or two later all alone
with just your motor bike for a conscience.
I've two of those & a speaker for a
light.

immanuel can't but sammy can

Put your foot inside the other door. Touch
the candle to the ulterior lay-away. Fold
gently the rocking lairs of harebrained
conundrums (on bass), zeroing in at
folds upon rolls of extra lather
(later). Then hum the tune
with a lingering sigh and coil
your cactuses into practices.

in between

FOR DOUGLAS MESSERLI

Debris – I thought as little of that
as of your hand covering it, as if
to do good was somehow foolsproof.
You arrive in discrete packets over years
and the composite is neither immaculate
nor contingent. Seek love and the winter
falls in your faceless naming, a
bill sent for recollection, attaining
a lift from a lisp. Go ahead:
live on the tongue just as you clam
up in company. The page splinters even
the address. Still, I've kept the cart, a
combustible dictionary, my out-of-condition
condition. Ultimately, link or cross
is less material than the pawing without
hesitation – how
can I help it? It's cold but
why bother with the causalities when
the war's never been declared? I have
stolen the sentence and now can't find
a word, just when I need it. It's
somewhere in the drawer. Can
you blame the arrow for
the target or the balloon
for floating away when you let
go? My brain's fogged, my mind's
lost interest. Whenever I go away
I know I'll be back, in the same way as
progress is code for
process. The rooms are let, the baggage
getting lighter by delay. The drift
has turned to drizzles in the private park
in the public square.

polynesian days

this is a long parquet fashioned with oil
where drove her ambiance. Mauve tangible
in equilibrium the presence
or collision of day and of the oxygen –
permanence that we fashion
with the usage deviant of ocean perplexed
choices enmeshed

all to contemplate the attraction
of the lumination
the transcription and limping improvidence
under where the 'o' makes itself echo
of the conversation reflected in series
silence intact
where plunge in traction initial

it floats verbs to invert
the horizon, the lamination cruel, undecidable.
Who englots hibiscus & plumera
the touch vatic of slurs
pours the lectern
of corpses obsidian
& entombs the flight
combing a timbre of voice-
bled basilicas

& the lure. The regard attenuated
by climate
less colors (brief in their difference)
point of repair
indifferent. The motes
cue me "marked profusely".
Debriefed indications, echoes.

me voiced. Sitting dunked recommencing
the place of lapses
in the merged ointment

the prosceniums
of yoked polysemics

Voilà. Me voice it was
tender, the corpse –
belly, eyes, response –
"marvelous souvenir" of the mar
interrogates. The scent. Allures vent
Louis pacific a plot we find
mobile like an hypothesis
longing for reigns. The incumbency

Permanence clacking in the oil
(corralled calligraphy). The calm
"loin of two" me vents: australopithecine
certitude. Versatile, yolked deuce
point venal.
Permanence of the deluge of transcriptions.
Voicing the jaw, the lamentation crude
who efface the horizon. The table low . . .

loin of two, the yokes of burden
lax contours. The yoke ascertains
the planets & the ore soothing
of the (regalia), the attention southern
the visage & incompatible allure
the yokes pronounce "demented
horizon" – orbits. Lake
Seance.

orient

the choices inflected
of the usage deviant of motion vexed
the earnestness that we fashion
collusion of day & of the oxygen
in equilibrium the reticence
where drove his ambivalence. Mauve tangible
this is a long arcade refashioned with oil

nickey, turn off the lights (2)

Such sweet abasement in undividable
Swarm
Who spew & crawl – Amalgam
Courts either herself or its
Compare, steeled
By potions of caption –
Presumption's dismay.
Plunge – Else spool & be
Unstrung, abhorring motion, sedimenting
Thrall.

the age of correggio and the carracci

Thanks for your of already some
weeks ago. Things
very much back to having returned
to a life that
(regrettably) has very little in
common with, a
totally bright few
or something like
it. Was
delighted to get
a most remarkable & am assuming
all continues, well
thereabouts. Fastens
the way of which spirals
fortuitously by leaps
& potions, countering thingamajig
whoseits. Contending, that is, as
fly-by-night succumbs to
dizzied day. Bright
spot, stewed proclivity, over carousels of
indistinguishable sub-
limation. Say, grab
the crack, secure the
figs: monumentality rings
only once, then pisses
its excess into the subverbal
omnipotence of a clogged
throat (smote). Haze knows
a different diffidence
which dares not expire
like the Generals who know something
we won't cotton
to, but swing on the trees
just the same: an ant's blood crazy for canasta (my aunt
with the cherry-blossomed chemise
& cockamamy schemes, praying for
Zoroaster).

poem

Just a few things first
let's see
a dog, well for those of you not
from here – a rather common domestic
pet, four legs, tail.
I should say
the seasons in the poem refer
to the seasons in the northeast
so that fall refers to the leaves
falling and winter is cold and usually
gray – often
I will use the seasons
in a metaphoric way,
as you will see.
By glass I mean any hard, transparent
substance, such as what you use in a
window. I tend to use prepositions
to suggest a relationship between
objects, so for example above or
between; while verbs indicate
action – running, or perhaps
colliding. When I write *I* it
most often refers to myself, while
Dante refers to the fourteenth century
Italian poet, whose unsurpassable
Inferno provides the form for this
very brief lyric. Since you cannot
see the manuscript page from which
I will read the poem, let me explain
that each line begins with an
initial capital letter, imparting
to the work a formality and
decorum that I can't hope to
adequately convey when I read it
aloud to you now. I have taken

in several words from foreign
languages: *Pierre* is a French
name similar to our own
Peter; *tristesse*, also French,
means sadness, and *achtung* is
a German word meaning attention.
Two more points. The goat
that comes up
in the first few lines is simply
a garden-variety goat. And when
near the end I mention a green
chaise lounge, this is a couch
upon which I often sit.

like this

I put my dolly's dress on
I put my dolly's pants on
I put my dolly's hat on
and she looks like this
— Woody Guthrie

Sandblasts median procurement till spec-
ified tolerance – a gurgle a day
keeps the lineator aggrieved. Although
abjection never leaves you humming the
scenery when you enter right. Men
are from Macy's, women are from Gimbel's.
The shut-away was shut-in with shoe string.
"Keep those calls coming!" *This is the worst i-*
dea I ever had. Enunciated
or denounced, doused or detonated. Nev-
er sleep too long on a good conscience – the
world's not resting. "Both my Dads are over
six feet." These tears burn a hole in my pock-
et no bigger than the thimble on Tom
Thumb's thumb: big enough to drain the world. REAL
DADS DO DIAPERS. The map of Canada
reflected in the mirror looked like "US".
It's not the pan it's the burner. It was
a dream of a charade of a chance en-
counter with a pantomime & you were
wearing limes. **Let the hole out of this tub!**
I have put my order in affairs &
my musket in formaldehyde. GUYS LIKE
GUYS WHO GLOAT IN GUNSHIPS. *It's the lepre-*
chaun in you. Flush with days' inconclusive
display (forays). A month of Mondays. Roll
over Leibniz, tell old Descartes get loose.
She melted in the noon day sun like so
much Jello at a brazier pull. *New balm*
splints team. Fragrant chill imperils aban·

doned evacuation (evocation).
Make mine schmutz.

> Till the top spills off the bibliothéque
> & the ground is splattered with tattoos.
> Till Mildred mows the carbon slidings.
> Till marsupials metabolize Mill Rift & Vivian
> inventories the resurgent bumbles.
> Till insouciance corroborates fact
> on the ratcheting slopes of Mt. Interlope.

"Be quiet, dummyhead!"

Running onto
plane as door is closing, sitting in back
as it takes off down the main street of a
small town.
"And slow Joe showed his mother that
he had covered the holes in the contain-
er and none of the hot soup had leaked out."
*If I have to come in and get you you'll
never swim again.*
Sets the motor hum-
ming with garrulous incandescence.
Tum-
ble dry invective, as if you could re-
cant what you cannot sing.
*Seance on Tenth
Avenue.*
(Twisting tremulously in
the teetering tugs.)
For example, when
the trees sway in the breeze.
Fingered in the
line-up she forgave the errant witness
while condemning the circumstance.
As if
our mass culture inoculates us from
the need for any other kind of cul-
ture.
Slowing the way with trellises &
codicils, colloquy of inversion's

munificent paraphernalia.
Pumped up & then sucked dry.
                              Propriety
injures its own propriety; which is
to say the only good order is a
dead order or do sequins sparkle to
a tourniquet's timbre.
                         One law for the
lion & the lamb
                  is America:
an even playing field except for the
ones that own it.
                   Sorry when you mean glad-
handled.
      Unfurl the flag to corral the
nitwits!
             If a computer could talk we
would not understand it.
                          (Layaways wast-
ing away in the imaginary
dream.)
          Then again, two legs are better than
no legs at all.
                Floor it & then liqui-
date yourself.
                ALL FAILS FINAL.

            "Then won't you buy my illusions
            Almost new, gently used."

Laced with absolute grimace. If you've got
your wealth you've got next-to-nothing, good hedge
nonetheless. *Instinctively impaired.* At
Royaumont, the coefficient of sil-
liness was just around the hospital
corners. *That's the worst idea I ever*
had. In poetry, being off duty is
part of the job. Take it & pleat it. GIRLS
LIKE GUYS WHO GIGGLE. It's an irrecon-
cilable difference among us. Every
soul a rhapsody. Lost originals at

the tip of your fingers, fractoids of the
darkling kangaroo. A fissure of speech-
lessness framed by stutter of molten fab-
rication. Planting an idea in a
beanbag. **Schools are made to be broken**. Sur-
er than a pick-ax in an banana factory, implod-
ing swamps head windward. As if the galosh-
es could replace the rubbers, the goshes
overtake the rudders. *Tool and die* – thus
passes. A crushing croon squabbling with Brown-
ian inaction. "Go soak a rabbit
& then repeat that!" Terribly tenta-
tive, terminally tacit. *And if I
mention Warren Sonbert, how can I ac-
knowledge that his films illumine the shad-
ow his death casts, knowing how hollow that
is*. How his grace mocks the scourge of what he
refuses to name, as if to name hon-
ors. "The body dies, the body's beauty
lives." The song is not in the melody
but what comes after, in the space between
cup & lip. For we have been spared nothing –
but nothing is the one thing we might spare.
Bobbing & tossing in the crank. MIDGET
RATS INVADE PLUTO. Little by little,
no fooling. *This* is what I always want-
ed, to return to the replica of
the simulation in which I am borne.

the impunity of garden flowers

The soul is but a morning star
And the eyes are portals to where you are
Nothing questioned, nothing claimed
But the rungs on the ladder
The threads among the frames.
One day it's lost, another round
Rolling in tomes that sometimes make for ground.

The barber told the leopard to jiggle
When detained. The shepherd told the sailor
The croissants are much improved today.
Some laugh in jest, some disdain
Most rush about in muffled pain.
But you always ignite the fray
Come futile hopes, come salty haze
No tricks to learn, no grips to spurn
Just a dollop of hokum and an open lane.

johnny cake hollow

Xo quwollen swacked unt myrry flooped
Sardone to fligrunt's swirm, ort
Jirmy plaight org garvey swait ib
Giben durrs urk klurpf. Sheb
Boughtie bloor de dazzy dule dun
Fruppi's ghigo's gly, jud
Chyllrophane jed jimmsy's cack –
Exenst aerodole fump glire. Eb
Horray bloot, ig orry sluit neb
Nist neb ot neb gwon. Shleb
Atsum imba outsey burft allappie
Merp av ords. Een ainsey swish
Ien ansley sploop ughalls dep dulster
Flooge, ig ahrs unt nimbet twool
Begroob, ig ooburs quwate ag blurg.

the manufacture of negative experience

3.
My bread has some nerve. No
sooner does it come out of the oven
than I have to slap it for being
so fresh. My head has some
curve. No sooner does it run for
the patio than the lights begin
to jam, the commotion dies down
in the corridor outside the
farm administration building,
Randy & Billy & Bob grab a Diet
Lite with a side of slope,
the nerve doctors convene for
an all-night session on breaking
the self-help habit, I'm okay
you're not worth the paper you're
printed on, or I'm in deep
trouble but you never came up
to the surface after that dive,
lo these many years ago.
– Boy, that makes me mad. Madder
than a scratched eel at a
Crossing Guard kettle-shoot, tireder
than a Bel Paese cheese at a
mahi-mahi swap, more irradiated
than the Aswan Dam when it was just
a speck, no not even a speck,
a microparticle, in the eyes of he
or she who will not divulge the true
history registered in these yellowing
pages. O! the buzzing bee, the lilac
in its puffiest fume, o'ertake me
on the road to total intensification
so that I be
as puffy as she

who swims on hands
& with her knees!
Jelly, jelly who's got
the jelly, or do the eye
pop &
else not felt make swarm
as two-coat aisles
in winter lawn.

17.
"Unhand the hand," the foot
replies, "I've had it
with your cakes and pies.
The earth's too sad a place
for me, I'm off to
Balm & Revery."

37.
<u>The Task</u>
                    after William Cowper
"Ian climbs well and enjoys the
physical challenges of the play-
ground. His play's almost always
part of a dramatic social pattern.
He will very often say, 'I don't
want to do any more. It's finished.'
But with the right encouragement
he may be made
to take up the task again."

<u>Rhythm</u>
"David is eager for his turn. Although
he knows what to say, he's still having
difficulty being understood. In rhythm,
he remembers most of the songs, at times
the words being a lot more important
than the music."

38.

If you've got the time, we've got the
felt. A high flier flies
only so high as there's sound
to fall back on. The only road
worth travelling is neither paved
nor unpaved. A ball is round
only so long as it's not used as
a peddle. Genuflection is about
as helpful as cuckoo clocks
when it comes to improving florescence.
Northerners who prefer camouflage
are well suited to cantilevering among
rotations.

41.

"When I say 'no' I mean
maybe, probably not, what's
the matter with you?, do I
make myself clear?, is anybody
out there?, do you serve a
no-doze with your lecture?,
how's the water?, are you
insensitive or just emotionally
challenged?, brace yourself
I'm going to write a memo!,
what's that bulge behind your
eyes?, not so fast I don't
want to concentrate!, is that
true or did you hear it on
TV?, the Martians may have
landed but they're none too
alert if they contacted you!,
possibly I could rephrase
that but from the look of things
you'd be even more likely
to take it the way it was
intended!, take your towel off
my cremator!, belt me again

and I'll certainly see the wisdom
in your *weltanschauung*!, that's no
pastrami it's a piece of the Berlin
wall!, who're you kidding –
value – you could get it for half
that price where I go – less!"

46a.
You know the type.
Her favorite drink was a
"There's no such thing as
a Little Bit Virgin Mary."

57.
"My sunburn's gone"
Who took it?
Who took it?

"& the feeling's wrong"
Give it to me
Give it to me
In the eye

71.
So far so slanted, hypogeneric,
imbued with imprecise and
unfathomable emotion; bigger
than a wolf in schlep's clothing;
elementally misguided, rerouted,
renovated; destined for a date
with a one-way mirror on Brim &
Divide; kicking a habit not yet
identified, observed, containable,
sectioned, sorted, leveraged, locked
& loaded, light-headed; suckered
in the act of suturing chiasma
of misremembered particulate who

skulks unheard in the visible's
obsequious representations. These
were his credentials, along with
a bit of twine taken on board
in case of slurs. The seas were
stormy in those years, so that it's
hard for a present-day reader to
understand the mysteries of such a
tale. Upsalla stood over two lengths
tall in her stocking feet, something
Bentley could not accommodate in his
deterministic schemas of unfathomable
lore.

333.
Haven't heard a beep from the beeper,
a bleep from the bleeper, a bloop
from the blooper, a pip from the
piper, a bop from the bopper, a
fizz from the fizzer, a hunk
from the hunker, a blat from the
blotter, a whip from the whipper,
a bleat from the bleater, a splat
from the splatter, a whack from the
whacker.

334.
Give me water & I will learn to
swim. Give me hunger & I will
learn to starve. Give me sustenance
& I will learn to survive. & the
people heard & saw & wept that this
had come to pass. & so it was told
& told from one time to another, from
person to person & book to book.
& there was a rending & a crashing &
a gnashing of all things, living and

not living. When the one or many
spoke, there was all manner of dis-
location.

482.
Is the Pope Jewish? Is that perfume
coming from your underside? Are
you happy with your lot in life? Are
you vastly overpaid for your services?
Is there anything that scumbag jerkoff
has done for you lately? Is the space
program the answer to domestic unrest?
Is there a cure for cardiac arrest? Are
roses orange? Does the villain always
have to be the guy who ends up on top?
Are the rich treated just like you and
me? Or do you think that capitalism
will pull you out of the stupor you've
been in since the iron curtain became
just another rust belt?

501.
& the moral of that is: Better
a loose potato chip than a
hot tamale. & the moral of that
is: It is a rocky road that's
filled with bumps. & the moral
of that is: If you kill the spirit
in others, you kill it in yourself.
& the moral of that is: Watch the
slings and arrows & the automatic
weapons will get you every time.

788.
Even the sand is burning.

the knees have it

I had a double meter
I gave my father half
He put it in his pocket
Then threw it in the trash

Now since that time I've lost a dime
I've even broke a flute
But all I want's that half a rime
To bleat the denting out

the human abstract

the shortest distance

between two points

is love

poem composed for jackson mac low's

SEVENTY-FIFTH BIRTHDAY ON BROADWAY AND NINETY-SECOND
STREET AS THE TRAFFIC IS PERCOLATING AND THE COFFEE SHOPS
ARE BURSTING WITH A MAD MOSAIC OF JOSTLING JABBERS JAWING IN
THEIR SINGULAR WAYS ABOUT THE FATE OF DEMOCRACY

They could drive a two-ton truck right through
your conception of reality and there'd still be
room for the Army-Navy band playing
"Rally Round the Flag" in twelve-tone
transposition. I could plug a leak with a
whooping cough and still dance the Da Nang
Waltz in triple time on the surface of a Bic
pen, were it not that I got platinum
blisters. IT WAS CHILLY AND MAYBE
SNOWFALL, POSSIBLY VERY HEAVY OR WORDY,
MUCH TOO WORDLY. "What are you looking at,
you old huckey puck (hockey pock, lucky
muck)?" *Il Donc: The Donkey Is Ill.* As in
an ill pill blows bitter in the morning and then
kind of drowsy or hazy, cascading up in billowing
dioramas of diaphanous derivations – dead
ahead to macaronic torque. O! the beauteous
schmutzing of the burnished begonias,
showboating to no cheese in particular, a charade
(parade) of inter-intentionality.

Take off my socks
                    my shirt
        my pants
                    my shoes
        my bracelets
    my rings
                                my hands
            my arms
    Take off my legs
                        feet
        ears
                        nose

                        eyes
            cheeks
Take off my lips
                    my mouth
            my skin

            Take off my industry
            Take off my guile
            Take off my imagination
            Take off my felicity
            Take off my fear
            Take off my idealizations
            Take off my eloquence
            Take off my assurance
            Take off my mourning

Com(op)posing in the gelatinous shmues
of indelible deliberations and lurking
mesmerizations. Counting, then
countering the counts. To blotter away /
Total dismay. By way of reticulated
moorings, absent prognostication, elated
soybean futurities. The pan bets the spatula
that the ink's in the spool. Don't school me
and I won't tintinabulate your nanojective fuzz
machine! Fudge slide on the orange fedora
calls for redemption as barrel of mambos,
Latin Quarter, 1962. As if logic could preclude
moxie. Nothing times two / One thing
imbued. Cleating the gushes with pink-jet
intensifications: Discretionary panache
of the pasha of mint julep. Like totally
inadvertent – jerking motions, flouncing, delayed
flutter arrestation. *That's BIgelow 9-8300.*
"But the fight has just begun / Stand behind us
everyone / Your $$$s make our dreams come
true." Deftly doubting (doubling) the efficacy
of the lotion (potion, notion). Busted or just burst
open.

            Bright lily pads waving above
            Time to circle the wagon masters

Hitting a nerve with half beats and preemptory
perforation. As in 'innocent guilt', the quill
hammers its daydream patently (patiently) dug out of
mortification. "Robert Hall this season / Will
show you the reason . . ."

Low overhead

Low overhead

doggy bag
FOR OLIVIER CADIOT

have you seen my doggy bag
hate to nag, hate to nag
have you seen my emerald chain
hate to brag, hate to brag

I ate supper in the village
lunch at the lodge
if you don't give me back my
upper teeth
I am going to drool like a

man that once had silver
man that once had gold
man that once had everything
but a tune of his own

so have you seen my nodding mare
my lurking pony, my sultry donkey
have you seen my cuts and jags
hate to frag, hate to frag
have you seen my broken drum
hate to gab, hate to grab

the toilet seat is down now
it's there I plan to sit
until I find that doggy bag
I lost while just a kid

the throat

Behind every figure stands another
insisting to be seen; but this is just
a temporary lapse. *I went toward the sign
and loaded up*. It was so obvious
I didn't see why I hadn't thought of it
before. Imaginary pain began to sing
in my right leg. I turned around and looked
back. The shining silver fog
seemed to coalesce and solidify, like a
roof. Soon we were drifting
past Goethe Avenue's sprawling
stone mansions. A row of skulls
stood as bookends. I went
three blocks and passed three lamps;
but the thing I wished to say
instantly fractured into incoherence.
That was the point: the world was gone
but he was interested. And there
was envy in his irritation, just as
the edges started to melt.
A dense gauze of grayish silver light
parted as we passed through
and into it, reforming itself
at a constant distance of four
or five feet. *This is where I
dip my buckets, where I fill my pen.*
If the bottom of the world is its center,
then intelligence is Imagination.
For all that can be seen
is made of Fire,
a circular yellow haze burning
through the dark.
– I walked blindly across the lawn;
then, without thinking, started
moving back through the bright vacancy.

I knew the way, I had *written* it.
Bones and bone fragments littered
the uncut grass. I took six slow steps
forward into a gently yielding silver
blankness that sifted through me
as I walked. *She was still*
wearing the blue dress in which she had
died. (Either childhood is more painful
the second time around or it's just
less bearable.) *The empty bottle*
and the empty glass, the dangling
gun, the words printed on pieces
of notebook paper. For all their differences,
each seemed crammed with possibilities,
with utterance. He had seen the other
side of the absolute darkness into
which Vietnam had drawn him. A meaning
seemed nearly close enough to touch.
There is another world and it's this one.
The fog made that impossible.

anaffirmation

I am not I
when called to account –
plaster over, dumbly benched
the corrosive ardency
of blinkered identification.
To affirm nothing, a veil
of asymptotic bent,
prattling over-
tunes in the striated
ecstasy of an turned-
around spade. Sprain parkway
gulls its titular
horizon, & my growling
Zebra knows me just
enough to tip
her hat.

little orphan anagram

Little Orphan Anagram
Sitting in a tree
Bruised by pride
Abandoned to decree

common stock

Believing that fundamental conditions of the country are sound
and that there is nothing in the business situation to warrant the
destruction of values that has taken place on the exchanges dur-
ing the past week, my son and I have for some days been pur-
chasing sound common stocks.

– John D. Rockefeller (1929)

Trades that are
    injurious to
        climate – gradient

of the supreme
    effort to scale
        a thorn

that hulls us
    firm beyond
        bounty. Hucksters

rescinding voracious
    declamation
        hopes

of a
    pear, soft
        and oval

to the knot without
    tangle that braids
        the dole.

Or derring-done,
    sometimes seated,
        that stills

with pliant
    warrant.
        Scuttle

behind or before anyone
has a leg to
laugh off.

Grateful but not gracious
enough – flood
in the face

of moral insubordination,
truculent enough
to eat a

truss. Floor-length with
an irremediable
conclusion –

views of the flicker in which we
pilfer – klieg-light
origin, defenestrated

micropassage. I leer a bit
but don't veer
often, comes a

donkey with silver bells
to lean on
(among)

& the woof of the day
fritters away
in loquacious

aqua regia. (Never sold
anyone this. Never
heard the

curb.) Maybe forget the fly-
trap for the crease.
Or show-laddered

past 9-o'clock shadow to
the orient of my
unfolding.

(All as clear as
punches right now.
Sitting there.)

As perhaps falsely implicate, hap-
hazardly conjoin, whacked
joints to spin the

Adjacent. Or maybe didn't
matter anyway, or to
whom.

Efflorescent bongo – plunge, superannuated
penny loafers – *as if*
you could crawl

your way out of history.
One wish
appertained.

But the dead stare of the facts
cooled the discussion
of desublimation.

(Shook up
but
didn't tell.)

Blood is our esperanto, flesh
our *zaum*, who
have no verbs

to frighten away
the night.
(Nothing

but words.) Noting
more than
notice

trick of a clock,
club of a
sail – keystrokes

of dilatinous osmolality
shuddering against
the loaded

drain basin, trying to grab
    hold, in front of, completely
        out of

frame. Then fasten your dock,
    divest the maul,
        whosoever envisions

lassitude. Millet of swell-drenched
    pumping, maldisposed
        actuarial.

Or else become safety net,
    sulfuric test,
        of love-bent plaint.

the smell of cheap cigars

When I heard the learned poet
Talking of incunabulas and brioche
I drifted aimlessly, falling through the mirror
Into the damp New York night
Lurking with imperfect confusion in the
Meandering sing-song of the street

max weber's favorite tylenol for teething

You remember Lorna don't you? Eyes frozen
in target light, broomhandles ferrying
arrangements among star-lost layers
of hypnogogic snake-oil sailors in tigerskin
blouses, Hoosiers with names like Itsy &
Whaddyawannacallitnow, tilting until
the shred reed repudiates its spent shell
of an end-run round habits of burrow & respray.
Mincing lessons in transmission, exhaustion,
insulation, *insalata, enchilada,* estuary,
earthworm. Rollerblades without socket,
toast without tempestuousness, farms
for the spoilt & indecipherable; – scruff
in the blaze of hay-damp oblongs, surfing
on a wind of flurry and missed hurry.
I thought the hallucination was a billboard
on the information highway. Then
ferreted fractures from foam, fends
from fable. (She dropped the bill
into my lap, the will into our naps.)
Easy just junk it. Who aped magnolias in
the slate Spring glides & popped CD-ROMS
into avaricious ports of maximum
irresolution of all but the pulsed glow
of screen light, mystic paramour
of boomerang & sludge. Whose conception
of the spiritual was to sound remote
& pull the emergency stop chords.
Who stayed up all day humming tunes from
Barney and *Schindler's List*, fantasizing
a world free of strife & strikes,
cocoon of the happy goon, uh, er, guys –
ballooned beyond belief in order to believe
only in the idea of belief. Shredded
rays of this hurl's guile, blistering

on the scream. Fluffy
& then
fluffy no more. Erasure me
& I
spin back into the space between
the worlds, cauldron of indescribable
verses, beacon of rumpled
hold.

american boy with bat

the surface
        in the
    dalliance of
            flimflam

Your thud
    a shadow
            a
clump
  fawning   faces

  (s)lit

cover up me for i cannot myself cover

Sills solidify silhouettes, dusting
Damask for dalliance, calibrate
Inherent astringent who slurp along
Cassidy, lo, over yon fisticuffs.
"The bellicose longing for inoperable
Acrimony besets tributary
Iteration," gurgles the eviscerated
Epigone of vertiginous glaciation,
Ventriloquising mopey insouciance, trundled,
I'd say, in gelled vituperation. Where
Wanton bludgeon licks the leopard's stain
Ungrounded by the titled lark that lisps
Upon a bend. Voracious trust, encompassed
Lurk, the chill imparts, the lush besmirch.

echo off (use other entrance)

Are we there yet? *Everything*
must go, is gone. Slowly the rips
fade from memory, foment
anagrammatic tirades, saturate
pensive perambulation (percussive
reticence). My aim to
loop corners and franchise
agency – for exactly as long as
it takes to blow the candles
out inside all those
headgear.

Have you heard the one about the stalled
kaftan and the bumbling pulverizer?
The Bronx crane operator and the Lisbon
tailor? The foldaway recliner and the nylon
railings? Perhaps the crease is semi-
permanent. Perhaps the conductor erased
the links. Perhaps the person-in-the-street
gets aggravated all the way to the grave.
Though, really, really & truly, I could never
broach the subject with her. Nor with you
for that matter. Really, now! The very idea
gives me a sick feeling in the pits of my stomach.
What am I supposed to tell Mandy? Or, famously,
Albert? The drunk never steps into the same
argument twice before falling off the stool.
Perhaps that will satisfy them. Perhaps the rain
will stop bawling. Perhaps absolutely nothing
happens absolutely. Or maybe I'll take a shine
to that stridently narrow interpretation
of what was supposed to be a common project.
Project me, baby, or the skin around those shores,
well, hm, delete that intimation of mortadella,
chiaroscuro, bullet holes in the newly laundered
upholstery.

Note nonetheless
the gentle amphibracs
smashing against the
spondees. Respond please.
Or later that afternoon, taking
a walk, taking a lot more than
was being offered.

– Tell Mandy
to handle his own
sordid aspirations. I've
put my money on
his desperation outdistancing
a modest reserve of
communicative charms.
He's had a handle for years,
just no one to pick up
on it. Semaphores, like
that German job with the
circular detonators (denominators),
says who? Surely you prevaricate
or is it procrastinate or
did you mean that we are all
predestined to be stepped on?
I won't sit still for that
especially if you give me
a minutes's warning
before I shoot. The lilacs,
last time I saw them, were
freshly painted, but the President
had eaten too many.

Don't crowd me.

Okay, let's see, where was I?

How many fingers am I holding up?
& now? (See what I told you, Marv.)

Arms too short to
vacate promptly?

The fire-eating
pelican decided one day to take
a detour half-a-league closer
to the Mercator Society. *Turn
off that ratiocinator!* The
sequelae had hardly time to regroup
before the President called them into
action. Follow that burlap!
*That's no embroglio, that's my
subconscious!*
But the journey's
bridle will carry you no
further than the edge of
the repercussions you disdain
to rule out. Society may
be the inevitable product of human
survival – but not *your* society.
The truth in pudding. Wrestling
with circumspection, overrun by
rigor mentis (even a rock knows
the difference between permanence
and transparency). She sleeps
the sleep of kings having descended
to the throne just after systemwide
devaluation. Scar & recombine, split
& whimper.

> "The shore is pouring green ooze
> The foam is getting darker
> As I swim in the cold, chilly-covered sea"

But those red ones – the biggest
mistake we ever made in chairs!

Holding Essence Position.

I told my doctor it hurt
when I lifted my arm up.
He said, "Don't do that."
I told my doctor I couldn't stand
the pain. She said, "Sit down."
I told my wife I was losing my grip.

She said, "What grip?"

Or will you settle your differences
differently, beating scuds into suds
tomahawks into torrents of talk?
– Stupefying prattle for summery days,
shredding water like it was so much hot air.

> "The markings of her
> footsteps in the
> rocky sand"

Sighing a far-away sigh, sputtering
Words from a place not-yet found, offering
Hope in the steam between letters.
The lap of waves against misgiving's
Disclosures. Stripped to the cement.
Because self-love's no love at all.
Like language had a claim of its own.
But the sun never touches the dark
Nor the night change anything.

The biscuit, the roll, the meatloaf.

Nationality is barbarity
Cleansing the soul out of ourselves
Praying the war will never end

sputtering & then quivering &
oscillating – the *I* behind the veil

Circumstance not existence made me
(the eyes inside the swarm).

Tiny green dots spackling the dusk.

Insinuating the rule into the abdication.

Total description of nothing
Not a thing

The unit interrogates the integer,
the digit cross-examines the figure.

Typing *finger* to see who's logged on.

"Did you know you're not answering me?"

Did you know the fire was never put out
The soufflé's still cooking in the oven
The little boy with a shovel but no pail
Is ailing in the street without numbers
Or covers? Sultry exceptions to the
Glue of social fabrication (demotic
Sublime?). Kerning capital and despair
Vagrancy & honor. Honor as far
As you can throw it, dicing slices
Into the premonition.

There's no short cut to eternity, no
Excursion fare to the heavenly's databus.
Desire means less to me
Than a flue to gel its wings upon –
Torrential horseplay in a can of spleen.
Your goose is gourd, your curtains cast aside
& the tremor of the tunes is gush.
Like mice nibbling at cartilage
Ice cracking the surface (sufferance)
Device cascades along the spotted hyena's
Tail.

Liberal potions of emerald green lotions.

The tear atop the tapestry . . .

lily's dream

About Emma. We were playing in the
playground. & we were swinging on
the swings. & we were playing on the
merry-go-round too. & then me &
Emma went to my house. & Emma
was playing with me & she got tired &
went back to her house. Then we
saw I know Gideon coming by. Then he
came over to play with us. & then we
played & then all the big girls came
with some gum & we were running after
them. & then we were playing then we
all of us went up to the Indian camp. & then
we all went to everybody & all the
parents went to a fair with us.

continuity of affiliation/disabling capacity

Goes

as when

door, larder

deploys

moribund aim.

She polishes

the soot

that interrogates

melody, melancholy

as when I

jam the frequency

of mention of

things

better left unseen –

daydreams of a

ladder

perched against

intensification

betters

mystery's rotting elan

until

I hold you

far away from

thoughts long

deserted

on the freeway

of my disintegrated

plan – planes

of irresolved

irredeemability

denied access

to other

institutional

foreclosures.

memories

1. Grandfathers

The farm never seemed the same after gramps died
Grace kept saying, "Every life has its tide"
But to have his testicles cut that way
Even if he had done what, whatever they say

The corn grew high as a boy in britches
I loved the smell of the bulls and bitches
Motorcars and kikes seemed a world away
We thought we would always lounge in the hay

The first time I was in Kansas City
All the boys and girls looked so damn pretty
I said to my great friend, hey Joe, I said
How come gramps said we'd be better off dead

Than drinkin' the sweet liquor and tasting
        the fruits –
The muscles and turnips and duckling soups
Such that we never ever none did had
When, oh when, we were tiny lads

2. Heritage

Don't you steal that flag, my Mama had qualms
But a boy gotta have something to boast on
Crack that rock, slit that toad
Nature's a hoot if you shoot your load

Flies in the oven
Flies in the head
I'll kill that fly
Till I kill it dead
And no more will that fly
Bother me
As I roam and I ramble
In the tumbleweed

3. Tough Love

My Dad and I were very close
I like to say, int'mately gruff:
We hunted bear, skinned slithy toes
You know, played ball and all that stuff.
Daddy had his pride and maybe was aloof
But when he hit me, that was proof –
Proof that he cared
More than he could ever share.
How I hated those men who took him away!
Pop was a passionate man
Just like me
And I'll teach my son, Clem
To love just like we men.

4. Sisters

William Kennedy Smith
He is an honorable man
And Mike Tyson's
A giant in my clan.
The liberals and the fem'nists
Hate men and vivisectionists.
But when they want the garbage out
Who do they ask, we guys no doubt.

the emotional truth

inseparable heat
wheel-churned
stripped quick as
shake, slipped
under
a stinking
mandolin
shrugged, clashes
shifts, loopy
swamps pad
imitation tuck
swaying botched
legitimacy –
         clatters
loaned transposition
unnecessary drips
bars investigation
vociferous, ah, heard
enstranging
scraped ebullience
merely roped
murky spaniels
mute spooks potting
purgatory, belabored as
use –
    conspiracy
twinkles, disconsolate
unbudging

circumstraint

Syrupy sunrise melts into tuna
boat overcoats, pasty percolations
inventing Dolores Day-Glow Dusters,
dolorous depositions dead-ending in
chock-o-block dustbins, Saturnalian
paraphernalia. I, cloaked in modulation,
stutter statically, surrender time to
circumstance, serialize guise with
desperate, maybe even phonoluminescent,
assignation. Sourly as soul unveils
surmising the awns obstruct the tortoise-
shell tubing – electromesmeric marble
lining the crevices of the tub.
Cradling craters as if tools
could be tired, suds salvation.
Slipping slaphappy into coves of woven
warbles; flapping slantwise at filiated
cliffs, chlorine clemencies. Drilled
12 feet over protuberant inclination,
nailed to the aerosol layer on layer on
luting, latched to the filter, lulled
in the fructification of trimmed air,
thumping and redubbing (doubling) the
tiniest of torn tatters:
such slope as moors me, fluttering
on flames, flimsied of foregone
fortifications.

      & Buster & Sis
      Cappy & Flappy

– like ramifications radiating remedies,
where tumors load carousel indices
and the excavations don't articulate
what's measured in incidental occasions of
demand. Sleeping beside the border

of reason and resolve, mirroring without
modeling the baseless bellwethers of alarm
and album (augmentation) – musty mulling
in morose perambulations, petulant
boomerang girding Devil-may-care lolling
sold for two bits short the cost.

Heloise of the

light
lurch and heavy heave.

Boats don't duck anymore than loganberries,
their manes rough-necking the clicks,
titular tutors who ransack more than
kindle, then slots sputtering fans
where there ought to be sway.
     The genial jostling, the incendiary
spoke – alone looks like the only gear she
cares to peddle is long lost and better off
bottled. Or'd take popsicles to the center
of importuning –
     like it melts
     but don't
     flutter, plasters
     but no
     clumping.
Gown is as formality does, with no
alleviation, batters berserkly
when all the time the
boy with the molasses glasses
is whistling "Polly want a flicker"
to the snoring ashes.
     To get a cold stay out in a bowel
rolling your tongue in tune to the
turtledoves which ducktail (denunciate)
into quintessentially (to repeat)
blow-dry flame retarders.
     To command is to misunderstand
where listening leads.
Today's a toy
that hides next joy or

intermittent engagement rinks.
Silly as much as Sally
darts Spot on open lawn –
        Dick runs, run, running
out back clear past (the) range.
A plan for complacent relegation,
denuded of song or story. – *Only*
what unleavens dwells at adjacency,
the blind behind the melt. Goodness is
as goodness pleases – as in
"are you headed my way or just
multi-headed?", sort of cancer-fill
ectoplasma that the crowds are all wild
about this Thursday.
– Tell him
the Russians
were right all along
but we
never listened, that it
wasn't meant
to be taken that way, that
January
always preceded May every time before.
I know the difference, though I
doubt if you'd care to tell me.
The planet's on fire
and for just $195 down
you can watch it burn.
Death also makes
for good conversation –
on the subaltern
decks of Outer Galactica 282.
        Nowhere seen
        Nowhere withheld
it's just that the button (buffoon)
wasn't pushed long enough – or the
Cluster Officer failed to exculpate
Latch Operations.
        Hold

the tune right there – garbled
in the search or hazy for humming
birds in a microsection of swirl.
The incident encounters its effect,
the

I counted seven
& when I
counted again
I got seven
again.
Go ahead and count
yourself – you'll still
get seven. You're
going to get
seven until you're
blue in the face
& while you're
worrying
you're likely to
lose your grip
on even those
seven.
But go ahead
& count – count
away.

empty biscuits

Ceylon's ox slaked Mary's gourd
Cycloned to flagrant dawn, sat
Jimmy's plight on gravy sprain as
Gibes in fairies lorn. Shed
Bright blood then, doled dizzy
Frappes along the gogos gay, jug
Silo pain, good Jimmy's caulk,
Ensued irradiant flame. Say
Hooray bloat, say irksome slit, as
Nestling slights no gasp. Rail
At sum, imbue outset, burnt
Thronement merely pines. Then
Aeons swish in Eden's sway
Slops hulls in duster's flow –
Airs numbed till gab, obeyers
Chewed, blur the blur ingests.

if .gif were a place

& I the magic in her stew
the north whine abundantly
saccharine to the chew
old stairs like all the majesty
was theirs
to take a lark
or flare largely malingering
adipose aversions
went right out the *fênetre*
into the bowl
where deceit is not known
& the dumb dance in delight
in the roar of a

ruminative ablution

I've got a hang for *langue* but no truck with
Parole. You can't bleed an egg cream from a
Stone. And before you knew it the better
You fell for it, circling around the
Bustle with elocutionary muscle.
Like they say in France, each to his own goo
Be true, licking stamps till the sunset sets
Somewhere over Honolulu. Balder-
Dash, balderdash, with a slice of cheese &
Velvet sash, some Worcestershire sauce on the
Tumbling glosses, & a bottle of snake oil
For my roiling pen. What's sauce for the gander
Is gravy for the geese – if you can't buy
Redemption may I recommend you lease?

today's not opposite day

Can't say can't not
Overlay of marooned croons
jilting their masters with
aluminum spoons.
I thought I sawed a mocking berth
a wrinkled lawn, a floating palm.
Going nowhere faster than a
speeding bullet on a personal
crusade to quilt the noise
& make hems glide.
The glue uncorked smelled sweeter than
a carriage ride through heaven but turned many
an head in opposite confection.
All together on the
blinkering rip of fate.

Dust on the mirror, tain of overex-
posed entrails; Roy Rogers & Tonto in
cross-country ski race for the benefit
of ardent but indirect reversi-
bility; suspension ridges tumbling
down, fudge brown, my fair cormorant.
Throw that spit ball at me one more time &
I'll fold into the eternal vapors
of my maker's marks. The revolution
will begin not with a call against sin
but with a hankering for bootleg gin.
Then promise me a roll or a muffin,
a hole in the ocean, & I will wrap
it with twine & keep it with mine.

What's that thing in the tree?
Is it a robin or a bumble bee?
What does it mean, what does it see?
What is it trying to say to me?

The furnace is cold before it gets hot.
Melon is sweet but sometimes not
The lamp she burns with a piteous light
It's not time to sleep but it feels like night.

Readers are cautioned that certain statements in this poem are forward-looking statements that involve risk and uncertainties. Words such as "bluster", "rotund", "interstitial", "inebriate", "guerrilla", "torrent", "prostrate", and variations of such words and similar expressions are intended to identify such forward-looking statements. These statements are based on current expectations and projections about the aesthetic environment and assumptions made by the author and are not guarantees of future performativity. Therefore, actual events or performances may differ materially from those expressed and projected in the poem due to factors such as the effect of social changes in word meanings, material changes in social conditions, changing conditions in the overall cultural environment, continuing aesthetic turmoil, risks associated with product demand and market acceptance, the impact of competing poems and poetry distribution systems, delays in the development of new poems, imagination capacity utilization (ICU), and genre mix and media absorption rates. The author undertakes no obligation to update any projective statements in this poem.

Misery loves euphony
and always tips the head waiter.
I put my
claw on the lute before coughing
up the clash.
The spot on her Gap dress
is the scarlet
letter of the media's star chamber
as bait becomes
stitch in the social cartilage of
mystification and retrenchment.
Xeno dunks twice where Parmenides speculates.
"You should really
wear your hat because your head
looks red." The
soul's solution the heart's despair. Nor
touch nor taste

nor smell nor hurt. The Mayor
bellows down the
hall, "The only thing they really
want is more
blue laws." As if realism gets
us any closer
to the real, counting any closer
to encounter. The
more bytes exchanged, the more men
that are put
in chains. *But polis will never*
be the same
as police. There
are no words for this and
these are them.

Four score and seven years ago our poets brought forth upon these conti-
nents a new textuality conceived in liberty and dedicated to the proposi-
tion that all meanings are plural and contextual. Now we are engaged in
a great aesthetic struggle testing whether this writing or any writing so
conceived and so dedicated can long endure. We are met on an electron-
ic crossroads of that struggle. But in a larger sense we cannot appropriate,
we cannot maintain, we cannot validate this ground. Engaged readers,
living and dead, have validated it far beyond our poor powers to add or
detract. That we here highly resolve that this writing shall not have vied
in vain and that poetry of the language, by the language, and for the lan-
guage shall not perish from the people.

What I like is that it
gets deep right away:
not profound, over your head.

The principal of the remission of
Singularities obviates against
The law of occipital mooring to
Percolate the ammoniated
Quantum of ramification in ob-
Verse proportion to the flap rate of the
Differentiator. The factorials,
Or rather valumetric cadences

Of these factorials, substantiate
The assignable quiddities of ax-
Iomorphic qualification while
Dampening atavistic insurgence
Of flexogenerative allocations.
Furthermore, and above all, anecdotal
Sampling suggests an exponential
Retardation of subsequent protean
Aggregation if pharmacosuturing
Is strictly factored for its intervallic
As well as protosemantic incrementation.

You're not from here, are you? I mean
people like you always act as if you
own the place, know what's really
going on, understand what makes things
tick, as if your precious imaginations
or deep insights are more significant
than what's right in front of your
face. So please, keep your big nose, your
insufferable theories, your exquisite
predilections to yourself.

"Is there a phone upstairs?" she asked
"& do you have DSL line? I've scarcely
time to comb my hair & still need to
polish my chimes."

A dog bit a child on Lakeside Drive. A mailbox was pulled out of the
ground on Mulberry Point. An injured cat, still alive in the road, was
sighted in the vicinity of Goose Lane. There was a breach of peace on
Water Street. A Chestnut Grove resident reported scraps of discharged
fireworks and six sharp objects, possibly darts used with a blow gun. A
person was bitten by a dog on Elizabeth Street. An attendant at
Chucky's Mobil reported an altercation with a man who, after filling his
tank, made several requests for something to clean the gas from the side
of his car. A Chestnut Grove resident found a dead bird killed with a
small dart, such as those used with a blow gun. A homemade blackjack
was found in the town hall lot. A Grist Mill resident reported a stolen
real estate sign. A piece of fence was damaged on Whispering Pine. A

town ambulance struck a town cruiser. A man installing an electronic
dog control fence was bitten by a dog. No illegal activity was found in
connection with a woman holding up a sign asking for work. Damage
was reported to a door at Bob's Cycles and Stoves. Criminal mischief was
reported after youths apparently moved a picnic table. A Lone Pine
Trails resident reported trouble after he spotted a neighbor taking his
newspaper. Swastikas, inverted crosses, and German SS symbols were
found written in blue marker on the outside of the window frame at a
store in Fleishman's Plaza. An intoxicated person fell on the green. Loud
machine noise was reported by a Manor Road resident. A property
owner on Old Whitfield street reported his lot was being used by some-
one unknown. An unresponsive person was found lying in a boat on
Half Mile Road. A Clear Lake Manor man reported a missing parrot. An
unknown vehicle was reported on Flat Meadow Road. A 7-foot dinghy
moored on a pond was reported stolen but later found at the opposite
end of the pond. A sick skunk was shot on Tanner Marsh Road. Eggs
were thrown at a plate glass window. A neighbor reported a neighbor for
stepping into her yard. A man was found sleeping in the grass next to his
song.

Man standing by his word, women
and children kibbutzing.
The man seems immobilized by the
gravity of his position, the stupendous
weight, after all, resting on his
spent shoulders. Sparrow flies from
branch to branch, testing the inclination
of the trees. Rumor of contagion sweeps
through the camp, soon replaced by
infinitesimally flexible incumbency,
turquoise incunabula, varnished handlebars
of the celestial taxicab.

Not the God outside whom you obey
But the God inside whom you become

What do you see, Nonny?
What do you see?
A tune & a stain
Waiting for me

Will you go there, Nonny?
Will you go there?
It's just by the corner
Right over the bend

Who'll you see there, Nonny?
Who'll you see there?
A monkey, a merchant, a pixelated man

What will you say, Nonny?
What will you say?
I'm just a nobody making my way

peanut butter and jellyfish

The scissor that cuts the thread courts the link
Can't get no reception, brains on blink
For fifty years ground the gears
Worked the dog, cursed the bogs
Now, for instance, letters are charred
Some say cajun, I say marred
Sent a probe, got stuck in space
Joints are creaky, thoughts a fog
Trapped in the glovebox of a pale blue Ford
Or hanging on a tree on the other side of Mars
Still, I've put that behind me, pay it no mind
As I look for a boulevard to put my pennies in
Slacks gone sour, that's for sure
Have you heard the news?
They're closing the 5- and 10-cent store

mr. matisse in san diego

Take Aeschylus Boulevard 'till you hit Xanthippe
Lane & hang a sharp right into Parmenides
Past Sappho. You'll see a light at the
Orestia overpass; continue to Heraclitus,
then bear left at the fork that takes you
to Hermes Circle. We're at 333 Pythagoras.

By dint of which
I have feelings, throttle
estuarial fireflies. The floor
conjoins the nap, able
to point past mucked-up
bike parts.

Art is clatter unveiling
its soulfulness. (A run-
on sentence mentality & a beer-
parlor lexicon.)

For which is buoyant want detains the need
flaked out among a trolley's pumping.
Blends inexplicable as it clamps, care
to masquerade, bullies to
glub. As
partly send-up, partly
hosing warm.

egg under my feet

gOP thItS biG GOBBie bucket,
seLls lik reiNdeEr haRwAre
bUj thAz's na thwat poont, flin
ferg juS brEaGinG ab gez laSto
flubper. Whaz iz maze,
INtendant to dEep fray ap ferg
exum[p]les twishting the roop
off'n unt goatee's buck. Fogem
frumptious besqualmitity,
voraxious flumpf. Hig ick's
wippy. Schlrp, fluuted, pissy-
podded. Blukeron atootle
noncious. Ablum ndit
clupilizittior. Fuzz,
gandapper, fillbooninous
claavqwate. Elevantine glopps
chutdle millipex – fums, forgash,
furbotame, fumumzyizer.

low regrets

> Oh rain me down from your darks that contain me.
> – Sidney Lanier, "Sunrise"

"The marsh, my marsh"
stumbles out of
bound and usually
reliable whistle stops
of comparison or
follow-me-to-the-stars-but-not-one-step-into-my-backyard
flutes their way to
secondhand accounts
of what, in another
life, might be
thought. The slow
caboose, with its
weary
resignation, shuffling
behind flights of
untenable gestures, aspirant
irregularities,
"counting the seconds
in dozens",
blinking in jags
like the elevator without side
effects, or inaugural
stunts
bouncing off the scrawls of
(don't
ask me again)
fomented momentum.
  Till the toast is cold
  Till the baby finishes its bottle
  Till you buy me a harp
Shuddering in the bright sum
of midday, smoltering with
ice cream and frumpled sodas

sipped through a straw
composed of one hundred percent
carrot product. Beating my rugs
until the dusk becomes
storm clouds,
Kona coffee beans from Honolulu,
ziplock packagettes,
The Club antitheft device.
The goats pass
from view, the boys
skip stones from
melancholy hydroplanes.
I should have wasted my life.

it's always fair measure

If you call me I won't come – just
Stop saying I'm so dumb. Or quilts that
Stone alone would melt, weathered
Withers' tinctured ploy, labored for its
Seam and never stung again. Like
Breaks on shore that bear obsolescent
Burden, turned head to shed the
Lacquered unguent of traded struts
Withheld at caustic stride. Trouble
Needs no bump, makes its bed where
Languid lies all snares, arterial (artisanal)
Club on melting mires.

breastworks

My breast is
bursting with pride
to see my son
go down the slide

*

Daughters have I none
My breast is
crestfallen
I am glum

*

I beat my breast
I slash my thigh
Sooner or later
They're going to die

*

Close to my breast
A deep secret lies
There are worms in the cellar
The fiddler – he lied

*

When chicken breast is grilled
The chicken she is sweet
I love it with marsala
It's what I want to eat

besotted desquamation

Somehow summer seems suppler
Swapping sense for certain stumble
Sliding on soggy sentience soaring
Slip of semi-sententious sorrow
Slit sections cemented sideways
Sullenly slurred from sultry surmise
Mumbling manicly or maniacally mesmerized
Motorcyclists mimicking Mickey Mouse
Misers mired in morose miasmas
Moored by mutilated mink martinis
Marshaling muted might majestically
Lurching like lutes luridly lush
Laureled luster lips luscious laments
Lackadaisically loquacious ladling

Arrival arms argument against adventure
Almost airlessly averts advance arching
Around aroma anticipating autotelic
Avalanche advised acridly to attack
Attendant attitudes, ambidextrous
Asymptotes – alluring allusive ambient
Betrays borders bodaciously burying
Banter amidst baronial bombast bedridden
Beneficence bumbling boundlessness
Beneath bucolic-brimmed bluster
I insulate irregularly indelible irrigation
Intent on illustrative inundation or intransigent
Illumination: Inculcate – inured – indelible

Don't delude destination, desecrate
Delinquency – dusty desperation dovetails
Dizzying duplicity desiring daffy
Doxa or dumping deviant dilemmas
Decorously delight to docent deliberations
Dulled by dusk's diligent determination:
Guiding gutted girders guardedly

Girls glide in gusts for garments
Game of garrulous grumbles or gooey with
Gorgeous galoshes and gabby gimmicks
Outline of octagonal obligation, officious
Orientation, outsized order occluding
Ostentatious omen's offending offer

Enviable egress erodes exuberant
Elimination, equipoise erratic, erector
Elided – entering ennobled entropy
Exigently, exotic emergencies endure
Elephantine encrustations, embarrassing
Explications endemic to entelechy; else
Cradles careless cultivation, kooky
Contortions caked on crabby contours –
Clinging clusters clubbed clamorously –
Continuous claims coexisting contingently:
Cavorting cathected kaleidoscopes cantilever
Xenotropically, zigzag zestfully, xerox
Xylophonic zygosity in zodiacal zeal –
Zany zen zeppelins zapped

Furiously futile fictioneers fume at
Fulsome fallacies fabricated by fading
Fact-tasters's fatuous fakery foretelling
Fabulous forensics famous far and
Funnily forlorn flips flailing
Fortuitously in familiar fallacies flanking
Yellow yes-men yanked out of yesterday's
Yearning for youthful yodels or yogic
Yowls, yeasty yeshivas of yiddishe yokels
Yakking about yogurt and yowls and yarmulkes
– Yet you yonder – Yeoman! – yell, then yield your yawn
Quickly quietly quell quavers
Quit quixotic qualifications, querulous
Quantifications, quartering qualms in questions

Running ruined rhymeless ruminating
Reason racked rigor rocked
Rolling rippling roaring roaming
Rust remains remnant of rote
Refusal, rigged removal,

Remoter recognition radiant repair
Hoisted halting on harrowed hill
Hard by Hawkings Helmet held or
Hurled – hemmed – hymned – hushed
Heaved as hectoring habits heaped on
Heaven's hallucinated helm, hum of
Unbecome, undulate umber umbrage
Ur urges ultra unguent
Ulterior ultimatum: uttered, ugly

Tattered tarped torrid tumescent
Tangled, tongues trip tendentiously
Toggle torrents in twisted tides'
Tempestuous torment tagging tipsy
Touch, tucked tapes, tossed
Tips: tugging turning tilting
Vaulting vexing vying verging
Venomous verdure visible vibration of
Voracious velocity, viscous value
Voiced in vane volumes (vexing
venture venting vapid voids) –
Jagged jolted juiced judged
Jellied joyance jams journey
Generous – jarring – jittery – jaded

Never no-way neither none nixed
Nor nulled, nasturtiums numb
Narcotic nebulas numinous nullities
Named Nimble Nester Nascent
Nonce's noisome narrative nefarious
Numbers numbed by nasty nearing
Plunked promptly into potentiality, porous
Pots plied from pesky plexi
Pickled in punch, potent penance
Penned by petulant protrusions prompting
Whacked-out wedges, waxwork wizards
Wired webs: wasted woolly wails
Wondering where the whittle wends

o! li po!

My Murphy bed is rusted
I took it to the store
They charge me $50
Won't see that cash no more

contagious proximity

I've had it with dolorous pre-
Clusions, deliberate delirium,
Miscreant ovation. The tuck
Salts the Bowie knife in the per-
Jured conjecture of an entirely
Forgotten antimony. Tommy knows
Exactly when to close his mind
But the signal's broke the other
Way. Then tip the deck of the old canoe –
She's bound for stirrup & Kalamazoo.
Don't let each fragrance slip away
To curtained towers in hooded bays.
Yes had it with derived delights
Give me wakeful implosion beside.

windows 95

FOR LOSS PEQUEÑO GLAZIER

Least ways barbarous

intent plows through

the imaginary surface

of a bulimic

insomnia, autopilot

isotope of the laryngeal

brace, inoperable

chiasma

beading a path

to festering numeraries

(oases)

hard by shaken

not fixed

pinot blanco

You can't sell the store if you can't sell what the store sells or else you'll sell the store short. It's no use lining your pillow with cannon fodder when in the next sentence the pigeons are pontificating on the merits of plutocracy. For when the Short Hills podiatrist says to exculpate the shellfish you know it's time to reamortize the leitmotifs.

Do trees breathe? Why are happy endings so lonely? Can poetry stop being poetry and still be poetry? Do birds suck the same air you or I do? Desire distends its own desire, fully as much as shade precedes shade. Glory in the preposterous imponderability of blanket denomination, as when a squirrel gnaws its ruts.

Now I want to repeat the experience I missed on retreat.

Slowly but surely I felt a rumor in my pain (succor in her refrain, a groomer in my brain). As for instance salt tastes salty, pepper hot, sugar sweet, apples tart. Yet while I remain unfamiliar with the habits of rabbits or the moods of mice, I shall never shake the knowledge of the bliss of fish and the despair of pairs.

She pierced my heart like blanks firing at the edge of an icy precipice.

Littered with ambient sorrow: fallen arm bands lost on the bannister between the mezzanine and ground floor. Like the suture congratulating the sullen ruse? A nickel bag for a 5-gig fix.

Then again, a false sense of security is better than no sense of security.

Evidence procured is evidence suborned. (Eva dances with portable oxygenation.)

"When Grandpa dies, does that mean I get another Grandpa?" When the hay is sold does that mean the farm will be free from the fear of foreclosure?

Ferries to and from the cherries.

So gallant, so indescribably furious. As from a fountain top, with roses for cormorant drops.

As if you could tincture time without collateral calcification.

It's as easy as a brick. Both feet planted firmly in etherization buffer.

Whose roots these are, there, afar, with a whistle and a sigh and a hey nonny no.

my god has an attitude problem

Being splints
it being hard
being Being
going on being
Being
being face-to-
face with Itself
rendering Its
rent replicants
rootless
writhing in
incontinence

the holler

Elude loins
in the
corrupt retention
not the cipher
nor the morphospasm
but the mountebank
in its own shelf's
malleable
tumble
drew back
and reassembled
with blank knowing
goofed
suspicion
in the travail
made foam.

the inevitable flow of material things through the pores of the years

Bleached
to the point of
subordination
blasted
stochastically
in the increase
of manners taken to
calling
COMMENCED BLAZON
surreptitiously trips
resolute
tourniquet
guiding the lackadaisical
flurry
(improvisatory hindsight)
chugging
beanbag apocalypse
interlineated upon
systematic
(or did she say systemwide?)
malfeasance
gumping up the
animation emulator
not a minute before
toking on toxic
thought detectors
tossed together with
targeted segments
of remorse, the
motive for infinitesimally
orgasmic
liquid labors, clutched
ordinances dancing on
head of a

whining for
Mercurial acrobatics, phonocentric
disquisition. *I*
mend the tense
so the lore may
open,
fiddle with keys
to find cues
or is
deputation
allergic to
elation, mirroring
churl on its way
to stippled
evisceration.

After
the crash
the
closest
we get
is
still too
far
&
words &
speeches
don't amount
to
a hill
of cream,
dreaming
an end to
scores,
a land below
the
flakes.

By my clock
it's ten to
& the minutes
burn a hole
in my
socket, the
seconds scar
a moment after
gone
but wayward
knows no way
than toil's
triumphalist
deflation, tailoring
tokens to
abutments, tug
to tissue.
The lowliest
incursions
are marbled in
fume of
doing's dated
demotion (demolition)
crawling
toward the
crossed souls
of delay and
infusion.
Millions more
proclaim
all that they
defame – defining
polis by
madness,
common fact
by its
disdain. Once
there was
a plate, a hat
I gave it to my love

with spins & claps
but quick she
put it
far away
now
neither can we
find
to put them
on a
tray.

Less light, less light
So we may lurking go
& go atumbling to the glen
& come astumbling home again
For Felix & Emma & Jane
Have scarcely had time for blame
The march, long march to history
Has cast its shadow too far to see
& we in the haze go foundering
As far as dusk is deep
We in the glaze go floundering
& foundering sound the leaks

Waiting in line
at square restaurant
with round tables
oval windows
sky keeling
turvy topsy
yearning dissuasively
for the violas in
plaintive view
as society turns them
(everyone)
into monikers of not-sure-
what-to-do-next, certain
enjambment, virtual
expiation. "I don't

know what you
mean" "Never heard
of the pie" "Close
the closet" "Bring your
anti-dousing lip gear".
Solo flight to
expectation, illuviation
ill-illumined
quagmire.

You be the monster
I'll be
bountifully unresplendent in my
taffy-boy alligators
or
lull-me-with-a-bazooka
mint concatenations.
You be
cyclic necessity
before I take off to
overblown barrage, cuddly
tutelage, encephalic
twisters. Torched
but never
touched, saddled
with torque
(torso) of
history's elephantine
grunge (grudge). Toot
toot! No
telos – no
turkeyshoot, bombastic
(emblematic)
erasures, strip
pining. Gurgle against
dusk, put a
flume in the
goggling
apparatus – hazelnut

boom in micturating
cadavers of
mottled obliquity and
fractal
obeisance. Foam
let me foam
among the crumpled
locks of dismay's
store – the shellack
of diligence (dissidence), the
garage without entrance.
Such spray as might
bilk a mannikin,
tangle with a
dweeb. Crucify my
makeshift allowance, derogate
the hole in this
rustic avalanche of
unadulterated
charm. Beside the bottle
is the periwinkle
in sync with
blinding arbitration's
two-bit architectonics.
Betray the doily
and sunder the
swift limp of
interpolation's bogus
village. Jillions for jihads
but not one
red fence for
occipital
invagination, hydroponic
telekinesis.

Can something be
sort of
or does it have to be
yes or no

highly or discombobulated
bilious or acridly
ripe for fulmination.
If the circumstance allows
she'll recalibrate her
orbit and pass within
nanoseconds of our
outer utterance, the one
with the wigged
obelisks and shard-skin
bona-fides. Ugh! the tolling
of the turbans, the bluster
of the warps. Oops! the syncopation
of the doldrums, the
cantillation of inordinate
inherence. Yippi yi eh
yippie ey oh! frisked the
earls and made them
brisket on rye. Forty
cents, forty cents
& not a second more.
I'll be there in
blink o' inch
soon's the ink's
a sigh – soon as
the ink's a sigh
my friend, & the rain
has a pocket to
put it in.
Then I'll come
jagged & I'll come
jigged
into the higgletty piggletty
rig!
*
Yes, forty
dents, forty dents
& not a minute more.
I'll be there in a
squint & a pinch

soon's the link's
a sigh – soon as
the link's up high
my friend, & the pain
has a locket to
put it in.
Then I'll come
ragged and I'll come
wigged
into the piggletty higgletty
jig!

hoods and scatters

Burns all over
but no pain. Must
find a way to cover
with paper. This time
will be the last
time, still again. And
not another neither. Like
tin can kicked
along the street 'till
it was only a glimmer
in the little doggerel's
eye. Or sail to Hook
& Ladder, field day of
the heliotropic monkey
wrench, bobbing in the
available disk spatialization
looking for the day between
yesterday and tomorrow.
Riddle my body with
tiny green holes, swift
flowing churls, inordinately
lacquered furls. Take me
over in a boat of
bent nails. & I'll
tell you a story in
the morning.

these horses do not move up and down

Dialogue's a dream from which
We cannot wake. The dog sniffs
Dirt to see if there is some mistake.
Little by little crowds gather round
Teapots explode, asterisks expound.
The silly sailor says to us the ship
He built is broke, Heaven help the
Nincompoop who shakes instead of bloats.
Take two steps forward, you're halfway there
Xeno's laughing, watch your bag!
Eyes in terror seek the shade that comes
Like buckets of lemonade. The bridge you sought
Is torn; no matter, never mind. Try the tunnel
Anyway – take a break, build a flake.

the stepmother's hunger

Bags away the laundered sleeplessness
that even habits awake in little
boys: a pony for the price of
utter disposal, monkey playing
funny bunny to the chocolate
malted exemplums. Grade the portions
with notions of endocrineal
implausibility. The grammar
is still extant but the hurly
burly way overstates it.

THIS US IS ONLY
WHAT WE POUR
ON OURSELVES WHEN
WE DECIDE TO
CONTAIN THE COST
OF OUR
FORGETFULNESS

ms. otis regrets

Can all you may. Slow th' ineluctable ruffle you

Proclaim as flight 'gainst bouts of bluster, scathing

Enhancement retrofit to whisper's motorized deputation

Gone and sunk its fizz in trios of swath, blisters

Of somnambulant concatenation.

                                 . . . where on

a grill some fifty feet above the cascade, its tremulous

lisps no more than hairspray to the sonorous inevitability

of your August charms, trapped not by the words

but by the thought of words,

                              I manned

the slips with such

lack of locution, enviable

crush, balsa

fretwork, unstable bounce

, that

never was known to prey on such

resplendent undress to

          The tipsy flutters
          Of last week's mutters (.)

I've dreamed the dream before

but never with the same torque,

increment of incredulity's

nefarious epoxy. Silhouetting a freeze

even the sift looks good

compared with –

"Could you /

pipe it / down / just a /

  crack?"

(Clinging

  to the old tunes

as if they were

  the only tunes,

the old ruts

  as if they were

the only

  ruts.)

      "My heart is beating to despair
      If I have to share
      I will be very disorganized"

    RAINY MONDAY

– No hole down there!

    TOXIC TUESDAY

– Hold onto that spare!

    SENTENTIOUS THURSDAY

– Get a reel and a lope!

    HYPOTHETICAL SATURDAY

– Where there's life there're spokes!

Which only compounds the problem which

anyway you've brought on yourself.

Only this series of duds, repetition

of promise long-since recollected

insistently ambushed but without

decor – you know, blundering

through the bagels and donuts

& underwater hoops or hatches.

The day was far gone before

a drooping salubricity descended

well atop the tweaks. Like

there's money but no investment

cola but no

frappes.

Learning to apportion hollyhock

and blued cheese, bundle

and tarry. *Simply the simper*

of surrender, hid in mutacious

mumbles. Ah! the stoke of

warble-scented stares,

encomium of nestled bleat

in privy diadems; the thud

of prismatic inscription on

a precipice of superannuated

cuff. Turn down an empty

sleeve and whirl the tumbler

onto the street. I've known the cup

but not the bearer, who hearing

only streams refuses lack

who nearing only beams

oscillates the flounce & flutter

of unsupportable (insuppuratable) fund

(foundation).

Few

and then fewer still become us

all – midget divers on the

planet of the drapes. So

veer no more my laddies

for the incontinence you fear

has overtaken the drive shaft

and the hole in your mouth needs

to lay about and untie its pockets

of melancholic spleen. Turn away

& not a day will falter, not a

scrim be grim. The fever

o'ercomes the fervor for

mercurial bust, architecture of

radiant supposition.

He had

a bug

in his

databus

flotsam

in his

file allocation

table

a glitch

in his

user ID

simulator.

                    Then would you

                         rather be

          a citizen

               of America

          or of the

world?

                              & if the world

     won't have you

          will you make another?

     & if the world you make

  fails you,

          or you

     it,

  will you make

          another

yet again?

Shutters shut and so do

          flags. Flags stutter and so do

     wings.

*I gave my love a winch He slew
me with his guile The storm is
spent, bills are sent My mud
too wet to dry. Lore is lent
meanings meant Silt is on the
tile. Trouble's near, it taunts
and veers My love goes for the ride
Thoughts appear, they vault and
jeer My love she slides the tides.*

Playing "monkey in the middle" without ever

knowing where middle is. Anyway, not

the kind of music *I* would listen

to. Billeted by the Bible the bullies

battered their way to Apoplexy. The orderlies

stood by as the accelerating carts sought

their species-essence. Everything

worth knowing I learned at

the Power Mill. *Don't*

make me / say it / again:

No splashing unless the person wants

to be splashed. He was so

broken-hearted that no words

could explain his jocose manner. *How*

many times do I have to tell you

to stop it! But that wouldn't take

into account the china set or Bill's

laundry, would it? *Flew*

then flew out of the room

& into the spraycan. And another thing

too! & so with heavy hearts the villagers

converted the pump into coaxial fable.

Now you're cooking with mashed potatoes!

"I never dreamed

I'd be here

with all you

slippers!"

Absolutely no percolating beyond this point!
Don't even <u>think</u> of process here!

The shortest

road

from transcendence

to

immanence

is

hilarity

What an unsightly odor! What a

sententious parapraxis! How come

you keep beating the languishing

azaleas or don't they have

interactive hypermedia under

the rock you crept out from?

You've got to build the bridge

before you can doublecross it.

— A real man would've killed that

bat. — A real man would've

fried it up and eaten it.

Wasting my breath (so much
helium in the prevailing
ether). "That's just not the way we
look at it here at Phisotext-
Montgomery." Cyrillic blouses
bouncing in the wind. As on a
lawn the light illumines
sheets of lustre, carpets of
custard.

              What is most real

                 that cannot be seen

           but only spoken
              in the jerking

                 firmament beside

              the veil. Song

                 that has no tune, prayer

              without address. Looping

             & then just scooped.

So much
morphogenic dirt in the folds
of the pluriverses.

            Ready or not

here I plunge.

the boy soprano

Daddy loves me this I know
Cause my granddad told me so
Though he beats me blue and black
That's because I'm full of crap

My mommy she is ultra cool
Taught me the Bible's golden rule
Don't talk back, do what you're told
Abject compliance is as good as gold

The teachers teach the grandest things
Tell how poetry's words on wings
But wings are for Heaven, not for earth
Want my advice: hijack the hearse

no more cartwheels off the dock

No more cartwheels off the dock
The cork is fried, the bluster hot.
Enmesh your fears in snares
& clots then tongue the latches
Of flip and plop. Ambush
Your furls with slack &
Churl, noting grimaces in
Stroboscopic curls. They break
Your shovel, then raise your rent
If it's not still morning it's
Way too late. There are marbles
In China I never will see, eggs in
Tunis, teas in Nice. $20 rabbit &
A reel for a rake, bet your bottom
Holler they're all out of steaks!
Made my claim long ago, or long
Ago it seems – fitted with a bedsheet
Without any seams.
                              Today I
look for votive lights to hide
the paths I've missed – munch
some suppositions before they end up
trash. The taste remains when the shape
is gone: Get a filling station & pump
until you pop.

frequently unasked questions

I've a pile of memories on my other
drive, just give me the word and I'll
configure them for you. I've got
the pearl blue organizer and the banquette
with double lacerators, but nothing
floral like those diphthong transducers.
Was a time I'd arrive decked to the,
well that's no way to establish
contagious proximity. It poured several
days in a row so that when the blimp
finally appeared we were focussed
elsewise. Later, much later, got
to cash in my gold for those new
chits – look so shiny over there.

inturpitude

Complacent rumors'
Molded deceit
Jaw of fungibility in
Nascent confidence
Regime paradoxically scrambled
Physically decomposed surging
Contrasts fauve hiatus
A key dismal Buddhist
Or tourist – harmony
Of Transitory pulling strings
Sprained cart is fragility
Prolonged order over
White fill – a sequence of mulch
Incognito, shattered, lent
For example, big cheetah
Combs shifting font
Occipital, operative, dunk

why we ask you not to touch

Human emotions and cognition

leave a projective film over the poems

making them difficult to perceive.

Careful readers maintain a measured

distance from the works in order

to allow distortion-free comprehension

and to avoid damaging the meaning.

make it snappy & that's final

Singly, then in groups, we file away in loops
Grateful for old-fashioned dusters
That seek but never find their luster
Or Spring the fate from out the wrong
Till touch is tapered, apprehension shorn
The gust thou art, the dusk become
Fluted, flickering, fallow, torn

sprung monuments

My bucket she is flat
My bucket she is round
Every time I close my eyes
My bucket melts all down

this poem intentionally left blank

log rhythms

Silly that sometimes, so often, the light
trickles into the room, and you move over
before realizing. Shafts and then sometimes
rafters. If only or then again, the problem
the lightness of the pen. Which lingers out
& over the triangulating trajectory of the true
or anyway truesome. I'll give you
a hand if you'll give me just a few
more dollars. After that it will be
every man for herself but I've got
the gun. Do I make myself insulate,
endometrial, inchoate, irradiant, bossa
nova, lindy hop, cha cha cha? I've got
a word right here and it has your name
written all over it. Hoops or hoopla?
Or whooping cough? Whiplash? Survival
without dignity that's one thing; but survival
without property?

My wife she stood with a loaded gun. Who
said that? There is no destination like
the present & the present is no destination
in the slightest. There's no destination
like the thruway either but I wouldn't
want to be on the other side. Break
a crystal and get a broken crystal – saying's
believing. Carried up fourteen flights
of stairs but rolled down only ten.
                Oh, do you know the muffled man
                The ruffled man, the tussled man?
                Do you know the muffled man
                Who lives on Dreary Lane?
Gusts so high you can see the sorrow fly –
and nobody know better for, or in spite of, it.
                Grill cheese, grill cheese
                Please don't make me sneeze!

> Heavens to Betsy, Hell-bent on proxies
> Don't let me be squeezed again!

Failure in the face of failure is no cause
for discouragement if you've lost your marbles
playing hopscotch on the canasta courts. I'd've
said that myself if I were in my right (or is it left?)
mindfulness, or mindlessness, it amounts to
much the same thing when the sum's up
and all the lard is spilled on the lampshades.
In fact, there will even be some leeway,
just after the bend in the mill. Yes the same
Mill who said it would all be al-
right if we utilized our mental
resources in an ethical manner, just missing
the mark by a gold bar. Capitalism may not
be destiny but it sure feels like it. Then again, weak
thought may not get us out of here but at least
it doesn't upset the stomach, while strong
thought is too difficult for its own good –
you can't leave the theater humming the critique.
The problem may well be the family, the bourgeois
nuclear family, but like the depo' man says,
"The family's the only thing we've got."

"We're all serialists now," said the barker for
the Language Contortionist live act on the Net. "Words
bent and mangled beyond belief, syntax twisted to
an inch of sense by our grammar-defying, double
jointed linguabats, who speak out of both – all three –
sides of their mouths & through their heads too!"

> Give me malteds, give me malteds
> & a turtledove beside
> An AmEx card for the nursery
> & a ticket to the Panopticon ride

Slimmer than the month of May, she pumped that
Rig so hard, hardly a place for a thingama-
Jig or a porcupine with way-cool guile
The mirror in the apartment glowed but it did not
reflect, at least not the thoughts that went through his head,
whoever he is. Dampness enveloped the place,

like one of those wooden sentries outside an old movie theater,
but didn't seem to touch anything, so that
he persisted in believing that the light
that failed could be fixed with a fugue.

"Nothing suits us like our union suits." Who
said that? Nothing suits us like our union suits
unless it be our transnational identification with
the flows of capital, with products not
producers, with UFOs but not ULPs (unfair
labor practices). The alarm bells sound and
everybody's dancing to their beat while the
captain tests alternative frequencies from the
bank vault, fifty feet below the sea floor. Dig
we must to keep from being buried alive. Where
there's life there's Coke and where there's
Coke can Dr. Brown's Pluri-Cola be far behind
if you'd just let me take the reading skills
test-preparation course instead of making me waste
my time with all these books you're always
foisting on me, like so many greasy french
fries from a '70s-theme coffee shop.
"Another 20-ounce frozen pineapple margarita
with a side of simusoy fish-bit fingers, sir?"
Just one more week at Reprobate Station, before
another week at Reprobate Station.

I've faxed you, e-mailed, left a message on the machine,
sent you a letter, & you still don't seem to get it.
Your routine is my Gatorade, like the hen
coop you call your gray matter, you know,
upside your nasal canal. To you localization just
means another franchise location, – location?,
sure, or you'll fall off and find yourself
paddling on all fours, if you can count
that high. You give intuition a bad name –
your instinctual response invariably ends up causing
the most harm, especially where least intended.
Your idea of morality is to drive a cement truck
to a homeless shelter. But, like my gastroenterologist
always says, the shortest distance between two points

is to sit down and wait till tomorrow
when you'll have any number of other chances
to find something else to do.

Now let me tell you what you really mean.
You're still not listening. And the loquacious
wit you call logorrhea stopped ticking
before we emerged from the primordial ooze
to what you dignify with the name species. It
doesn't take a genius to see that if you don't
keep the slide on the pot all the butter will
spoil away. It doesn't take a weatherman to
know that an ill wind needs head rest and plenty of
reconceptualization. The stump don't work 'cause the
loggers took the cell phone. Just because
I have no advice to sell doesn't mean
the buzz saw's not jammed in the baklava
bush. At least with an infomercial you know
where they're coming from. Just because
redeployment had been pushed back till opportunity
stops banging desperately at the portals –
then get your own planet!

This is the story of the lox and the frown.
You can follow along with me in your book.
You will know it is time to turn the page
when you hear the chimes ring like this –
(•◉•)(•◉•). One day, the lox said to the frown,
"Let's buy some bagels and go to the town."
"I'm not up for that," said the frown, with a
discouraging leer. "What do you say we just
stay here?" (•◉•)(•◉•) The lox and the frown
had reached an impasse. (•◉•)(•◉•) "I know," said
the lox, "let's have a conversation." "I'm not sure
we can sustain a conversation," said the frown.
"What about the good life?" said the lox. "Do you
think you can lead a good life if what you do
does not contribute to the good life for others?"
(•◉•)(•◉•) "Depends on what you mean by good,"
said the frown, going out of his way to
sound disinterested. "Good for whom?

Good in what sense?" "For me, the good has
got to be the good for everyone, and in the
ideal sense," replied the lox, turning red, or anyway
redder. (॥ ◉ ॥)(॥ ◉ ॥) "But something that is aesthetically
good is not necessarily ethically good. I mean
morality and art are more often at odds than
not. It may be that the nature of judgment, not
to say taste, is similar in aesthetics and ethics, but
the ends of each is quite distinct." (॥ ◉ ॥)(॥ ◉ ॥) "When
aesthetics and ethics seem to clash," said the lox,
"maybe it's because we have boxed both in as
separate, even conflicting. Maybe it's morality
and ethics that are at odds, and by the good
we mean some way to recognize both the basis
and the limits of our judgments." (॥ ◉ ॥)(॥ ◉ ॥) "Seems
to me," said the frown in a smug tone, "that you're
putting a lot of energy into evading the fact that what's
pleasing to the tongue may be injurious to the
language – that the body has a different set
of interests than the body politic." (॥ ◉ ॥)(॥ ◉ ॥) "I think
I will go into the town after all," said the lox to the frown.
"Conversation can get you only so far."

Bob's Body Shop
Bob's Bait
Bob's Auto and Truck Repairs
Bob's Grocers
Bob's Ice Cream
Bob's Variety
Bob's Marine
Bob's Beach Miniature Golf
Bob's Billiards
Bob's Boat Rental
Bob's Camera and Craft
Bob's Camping Equipment Co.
Bob's Canvas and Upholstery
Bob's Construction
Bob's Diner
Bob's Hardware
Bob's Train and Hobby Center
Bob's Pool Service

Bob's Garage
Bob's Laundromat
Bob's Log Homes
Bob's Novelty
Bob's Pancake House
Bob's RV Park
Bob's Realty
Bob's Self-Storage
Bob's Sports Outlet
Bob's Surf Shop
Bob's Taxi Co.
Bob's Motel
Bob's Welding
Bob's Flag and Pole Co.
Bob's Gift and Garden Center
Bob's Awning and Tent
Bob's Used Furniture and Antiques
Bob's Frames
Bob's Auto Parts
Bob's Drywall
Bob's Hauling
Bob's Bungalows
Bob's Bearings, Inc.
Bob's Pharmacy
Bob's Leather Craft
Bob's Glass Doctor
Bob's Barber Shop
Bob's Ducts
Bob's Heating and Cooling
Bob's Roofing and Siding
Bob's Vacuum and Appliance Repair
Bob's Pallets and Skids
Bob's Septic and Drain
Bob's Stationers
Bob's Tile

How much longer will I have to survive on
Thomas' English Muffins and squeezeable rye?
Do tears fall if you don't push them? And
if you wake up in a field of macaroons,
does that mean you've tripped on the ledge or that

bailiffs are coming from the Argentine? I
know that the radiance before me has no
name and that it comes not from my
imagination nor some place beyond. That
each night and in the day you are suffused
with a glow that is solid, sturdy, contained
or then again like the shine of the sun at play
in the rippling water. It's something so utterly
ordinary, unburdened by mystique or the
romance of intoxication, riveting without
rivets, flush with the flesh of years. As one
sobered into exultation or grounded to a circuit,
or like the stew that simmers but does
not boil, suffused passion eclipses its
infatuated cousin, whose spiked intensities are
consolation for, or premonitions of, that fire
that burns but will not expire.

The puppy is father to the dog, or possibly
father-in-law, or cousin – in any case: related.
The mouse chases the cat but only in the poem.
Blankets of vermilion indecision plaster
the perimeter, then fade, like the row without
the boat, into presumptive disquisition. An
act absorbs an ax, or the other way around –
circumspection overpowering its blotchy neighbors to
leap with Nijinskian ardour to the layered
logics of its subaltern flock. Wending while
waiting, entanglement buffets its trumpeting
truffles with a gleam of gloom about the
pupils, moving up the shore at several
knots above pace. Or untie the bow
to release the box to its destined foreclosure.
The gift is always less than it seems:
Commodification will never compensate
for the empty package of our liveried lives.
If action is always compromised then speculation is
revving the engine before shifting to
overdrive. Lullabies reproach, laments detract,
the solemn songs delude – let language lead.

Where? Do not grin & fidget, let us
go & make our widgets. The journey has
long since dissolved into the solution, so that
when we shake it we see only the
disturbed sentiment that marks the abandoned
paths. Turn off the motor to light
the course.

notes and acknowledgments

With Strings is organized as a vortex, with each poem furthering the momentum of the book while curving its arc of attentional energy. The structure is modular: a short work might become part of a serial poem or a section of a serial poem might stand on its own. The effect is to make the book as a whole a string of interchanging parts. Political, social, ethical, and textual investigations intermingle, presenting a linguistic echo chamber in which themes, moods, and perceptions are permuted, modulated, reverberated, and further extended. "The Book as Architecture" in *My Way: Speeches and Poems* (University of Chicago Press, 1999) explores some of these organizational potentialities. *My Way* is a companion volume to *With Strings*; although one poem in *With Strings* is from 1982 ("The Age of Correggio and the Carracci"), the rest were written between 1986 and 1999.

"In Place of a Preface a Preface" is adapted from a discussion of the work of Arakawa and Madeline Gins in "Every Which Way But Loose" in *Textual Studies in the Late Age of Print: Reimagining Textuality*, ed. Elizabeth Bergmann Loizeaux and Neil Fraistat (University of Wisconsin Press, 2001).

"Ballad of Blue Green Plate" was written in the shadow of Baboquivari Peak, southwest of Tucson. Baboquivari is the home of I'itoi, the Papago (Tohono O'odham) creator.

"In Between" is a response to an initial set of poems by Douglas Messerli called *Between*, which were written "through" poems of his friends.

"Polynesian Days" is homophonically adapted from Nicole Brossard's "Polynésie des yeux", in *À tout regard* (Montréal: BQ [Bibliothèque québécoise], 1989).

"Like This": The films of Warren Sonbert (1947–1995) include *Amphetamine, The Bad and the Beautiful, Carriage Trade, Rude Awakening, Divided Loyalties, Noblesse Oblige, A Woman's Touch, The Cup and the Lip, Honor and Obey, Friendly Witness,* and *Short Fuse.* Sonbert died of AIDS.

"The Throat" has as its source Peter Straub's *The Throat* (New York: Dutton, 1993).

"Empty Biscuits" is a translation of "Johnny Cake Hollow."

The poems collected in *With Strings* first appeared in *Aerial, American Letters and Commentary, Agni, American Poetry Review, American Poets Say Goodbye to the Twentieth Century,* ed. Andrei Codrescu and Laura Rosenthal (New York: Four Walls Eight Windows, 1996), *Barrow Street, boundary 2, Carrionflower Writ, Common Knowledge, Conjunctions, Crayon, El-e-phant, Electronic Book Review, The End Review, Facture, Fence, Flash Point, Hunger Magazine, Infolio, Jacket, Kenning, Kiosk, Lipstick Eleven, Minnesota Review, New American Writing, notus, O.Ars, Object, Parataxis, Poetry New York, Poetry New Zealand, Princeton Library Chronicle, Queen Street Quarterly, Raddle Moon, Rhizome, Ribot, River City, Salt, Salt Hill, Slope, Stele, Sulfur, Tinfish, Tool, Valentine, Verse,* and *Web Del Sol.* Some of the poems first appeared in two collaborations with Susan Bee – *Log Rhythms* (Granary Books, 1998) and *Little Orphan Anagram* (Granary Books, 1997). My thanks to the editors and publishers.